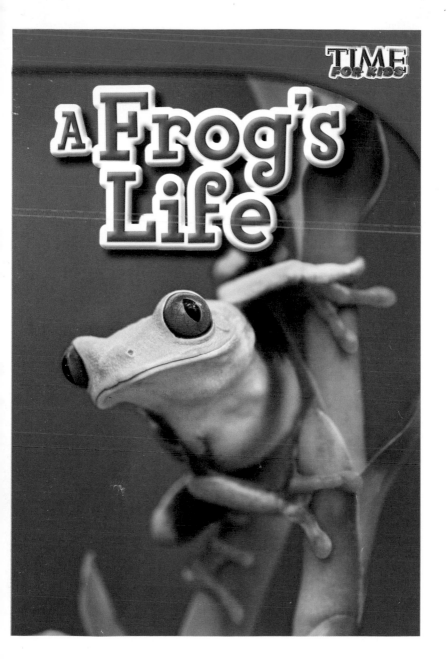

A Frog's Life

TIME FOR KIDS

Dona Herweck Rice

Consultant

Timothy Rasinski, Ph.D.
Kent State University

Publishing Credits

Dona Herweck Rice, *Editor-in-Chief*

Lee Aucoin, *Creative Director*

Conni Medina, M.A.Ed., *Editorial Director*

Jamey Acosta, *Editor*

Robin Erickson, *Designer*

Stephanie Reid, *Photo Editor*

Rachelle Cracchiolo, M.S.Ed., *Publisher*

Image Credits

Cover Mark Kostich/iStockphoto; p.3 Elena Elisseeva/Shutterstock;
p.4 Marek Mierzejewski/Shutterstock; p.5 Buddy Mays/Photo Library;
p.6 Dirk Ercken/Shutterstock; p.7 Kerstin Layer/Photo Library, Marius Neacsa/iStockphoto;
p.8 dabjola/Shutterstock; p.9 Matej Ziak/Shutterstock; p.10 hagit bekovich/Shutterstock;
p.11 François Gilson/Photo Library; p.12 Hans Pfletschinger/Photo Library;
p.13 Jiří Hodeček/iStockphoto; p.14 gosn.Momcilo/Shutterstock;
p.15 Cathy Kiefer/Shutterstock; p.16 Marius Neacsa/iStockphoto, gosn.Momcilo/
Shutterstock, Jiří Hodeček/iStockphoto; p.17 dabjola/Shutterstock, Matej Ziak/Shutterstock,
Hans Pfletschinger/Photo Library; p.18 Petrov Anton/Shutterstock;
p.19 Dirk Ercken/Shutterstock, Elena Elisseeva/Shutterstock, dabjola/Shutterstock;
back cover Richard Peterson/Shutterstock

Based on writing from *TIME For Kids*.

Teacher Created Materials

5301 Oceanus Drive
Huntington Beach, CA 92649-1030
http://www.tcmpub.com
ISBN 978-1-4333-3586-0
© 2012 Teacher Created Materials, Inc.

It all begins at the **pond**.

This is the home of the
mother **frog**.

She is ready to have babies.

She lays eggs in the water.
Each egg can become a
frog.

When the eggs hatch,
tadpoles come out.

A tadpole looks like a
little fish.

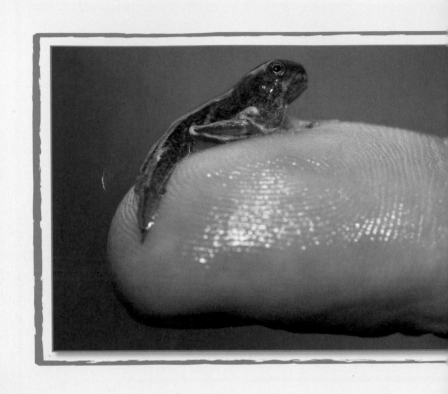

The tadpole grows.

It looks like a fish with two legs!

Now it looks more like
a frog.

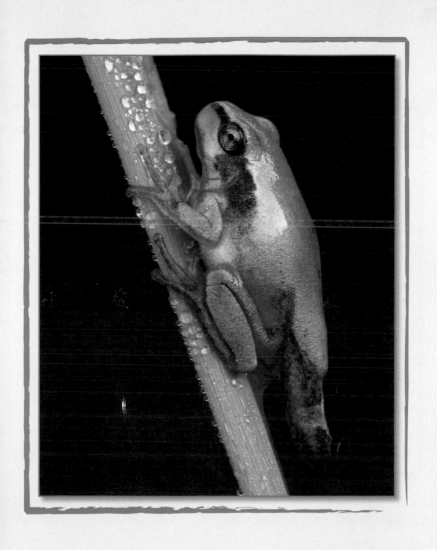

Then it grows four legs.

Each young frog becomes
an adult frog.

The frog looks like its
mother and father.

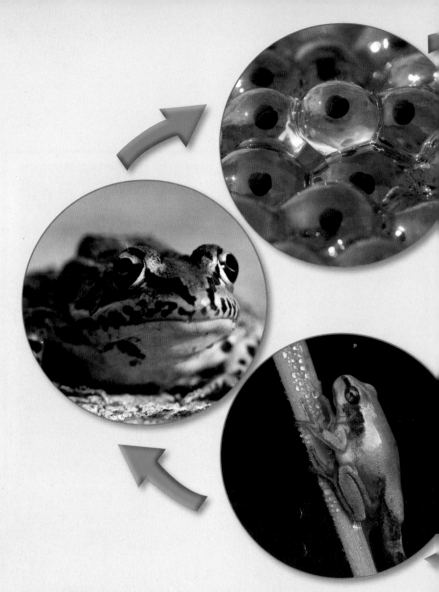

Then the grown frog can have tadpoles, too.

Everything will begin again.

This is a frog's life.

Glossary

frog

pond

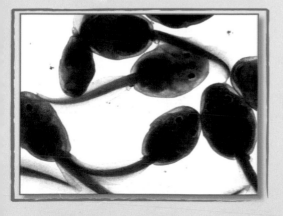

tadpoles

Words to Know

adult

babies

become

begin

egg

father

fish

frog

grows

hatch

lays

legs

life

mother

pond

tadpole

young